Witch's Moon

A Beginner's Guide to Moon Magic

Amy Cesari

Be a fire-safe witch!

Lots of space above and around the flame.

Candle is on a fire-safe dish.

Never leave flames unattended.

COPYRIGHT & GENERAL DISCLAIMER:

WITCH'S MOON: A BEGINNER'S GUIDE TO MOON MAGIC
ALL TEXT AND IMAGES © 2022 BOOK OF SHADOWS LLC, AMY CESARI

THIS BOOK DOES NOT CONTAIN MEDICAL ADVICE AND DOES NOT INTEND TO TREAT OR DIAGNOSE MEDICAL OR HEALTH ISSUES. ALWAYS SEEK PROFESSIONAL MEDICAL TREATMENT. AND DON'T EAT OR USE PLANTS IF YOU DON'T KNOW WHAT THEY ARE.

ALL RIGHTS RESERVED. For personal use only. No parts of this book may be reproduced, copied, or transmitted in any form, by any means, including photocopying, recording, or other electronic or mechanical methods, without the prior written permission of the author, except in the case of brief quotations for critical reviews and certain other noncommercial uses permitted by copyright law. **DISCLAIMER OF LIABILITY:** This book is for informational and entertainment purposes only and is not intended as a substitute for medical, financial, spiritual, or life advice of any kind. Like any craft involving flames, the power of your mind unhinged, eating plants and herbs, and the unyielding forces of the universe, Witchcraft poses some inherent risk. The author and publisher are not liable or responsible for any outcome of magical spells performed from this book or otherwise. Readers agree to cast spells, work with fire, ingest herbs, soak in bath salts, light candles and incense, channel deities, use spirit boards, and perform any and all other magical practices at their own risk. The images in this book are for decorative purposes—they are not realistic guides for arranging flame-based altars. Always place a fireproof dish beneath candles & incense. Leave clearance above & around flames. Do not place flammable objects near flames and never leave flaming things or incense unattended. Readers of this book take full responsibility when using fire. Readers accept full personal risk and responsibility for the outcome, consequence, and magic of any spells they cast. This book is not for children. And so it shall be.

A full moon ritual is called an Esbat.

Hail and Welcome to Your Magical Life

The Magic is in Your Hands.

The moon is comforting and familiar, yet mysterious and full of possibility. Moon magic isn't about becoming the best version of yourself, but about accepting all phases—dark to light—as essential pieces of you.

Much of the moon's power lies in a subtle energy where "all is well." But the moon is also about experiencing growth, change, and new phases in a continuous cycle.

The most widely accepted definition of magic is the ability to influence your destiny. When you use magic, you can harness your intention, will, and the natural forces around you, such as the moon, the sun, the planets, and the changing seasons.

Magic is like an invisible thread. You may barely notice it's there at times. But if you hang onto that thread of intention (and action) through the many moons and phases of life, that magic will come through for you in life-changing ways.

This book isn't about planning to do more, but about prioritizing magic in your life and pulling that thread forward with intention. So imagine yourself in a feeling-place where nothing is wrong and there's nothing to fix. You've already got what you need to make your life magical. Are you ready? Say yes!

Using Your "Moon Child" Intuition

Witches and mystics have associated intuition, moon magic, and the watery depths of the subconscious for thousands of years. So how do you actually use your intuition and the moon's magic? Here's the secret. (Try it now! It works!)

1. *Close your eyes and imagine that you are the moon.* Then look down on your physical self, a little "moon child" here on earth. Pause for a moment and just observe your human self from the perspective of the moon.

2. Let the moon see all of your feelings, dark and light. Let it see your insecurities, flaws, worries, fears, whatever you've got going on, and lay it out on the moon table.

3. From outside of yourself—from the moon's perspective—what does the moon see? What wisdom does the loving and accepting moon have for you, a perfect moon child in all phases, from dark to light?

The moon sees you without judgment—always. To love and accept the phases of the moon is to love and accept yourself in all phases, too.

When you see yourself as the moon sees you, you'll begin an upward spiral of energy, raising your spirit so you feel a little bit more magical, hopeful, curious, capable, or clear.

The moon's endless cycles represent the many new chances you have to try again, to feel a little better, or to reinvent yourself all over. When you know that it's "just a phase" to have both dark and light, you can hold on to that thread of intention and keep your magic growing by the phases of the moon.

Tips For Using This Book

• Notice and take notes about how you feel during the different phases of the moon. Everyone has their own personal "moon cycle," and we all experience the moon in unique ways according to our own energy and phases of life. Use this book as a guide, but don't feel tied or bound to any of the symbolism and spells. Adjust, improvise, create, and strive to use moon magic in the ways that work best for you.

• "Spellcasting Basics" are included to show you how to cast a circle, ground and center, and perform a "full" spell. If you are new to spells, please be sure to read this.

• Always remember, the magic is inside you. Even if it isn't "the best" moon phase, you are the most powerful force in your own life. The seasons, sun, moon, and other forces of natural magic are just tools to help you unlock the magic within.

MOON MAGIC
The Big Picture

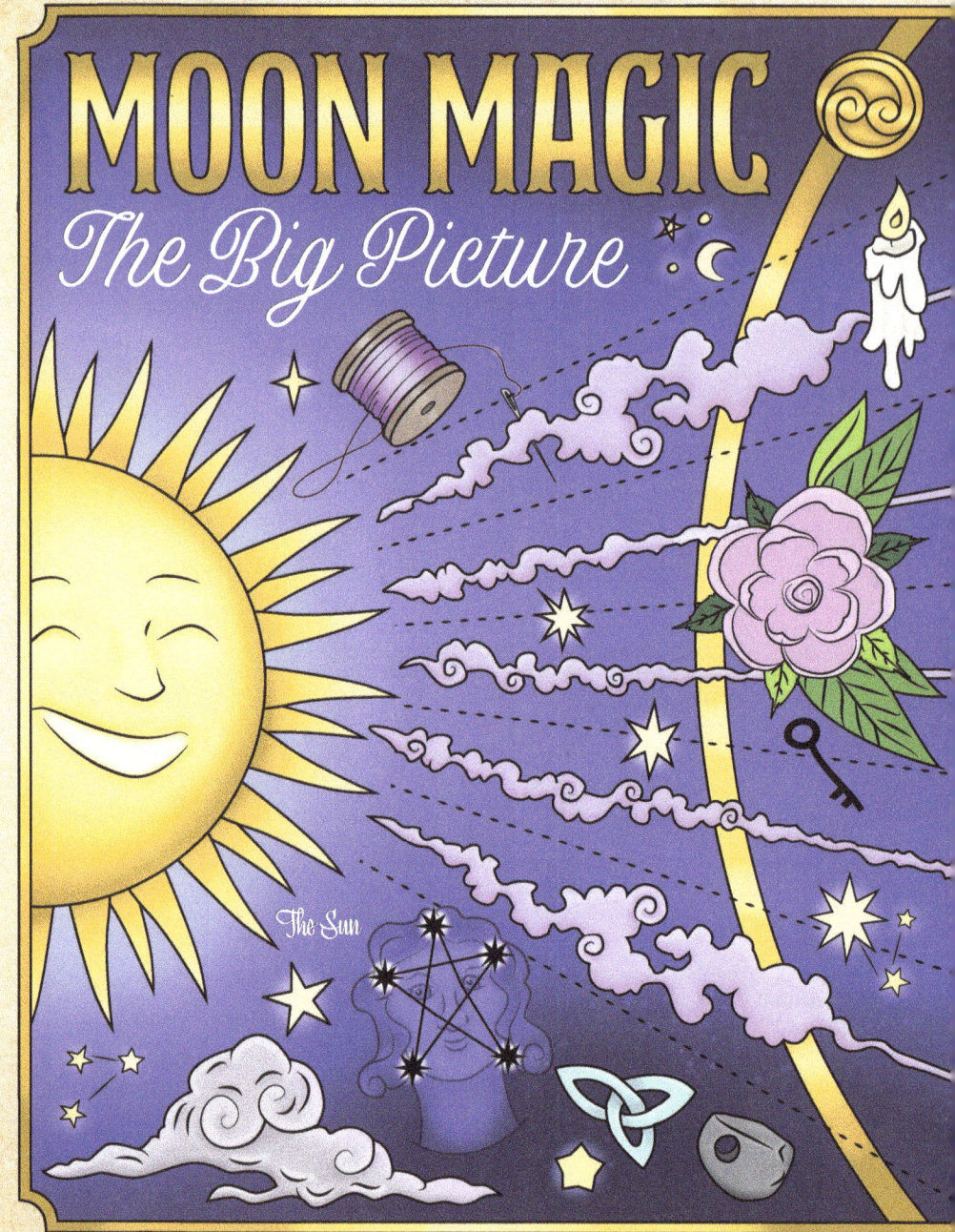

The Sun

The moon was likely created by the debris from a large object crashing into earth. And so the moon is actually a part of "us" (the earth) and also part of the cosmos—As Above, So Below.

The moon is a gravitational counterbalance to the earth. Its presence helps to steady out the climate and seasons, and the moon has played an important part of life's evolution on the planet.

The gravitational pull of the moon also causes the land and water to bulge on two sides of the earthly sphere. We call this phenomenon "the tides." You've probably witnessed the water's tides, but there is also a land tide that literally causes the earth's crust to bulge a few centimeters or more.

In theory, the moon's gravity also affects people, plants, and animals on the earth.

The moon "pushes and pulls" on the energy, water, and "tides" in our bodies and can affect our moods, energy levels, and subconscious—

therefore making the moon a powerful and plentiful force to use in magic.

And although the moon is often the brightest light in the night sky, it doesn't illuminate itself. The moon reflects the light of the sun.

You can use this metaphorical power to look at your own reflection, viewing yourself from a top-down perspective of intuition. (See the previous "Moon Child Intuition" exercise.)

You can also use this reflective magic to work with manifestation and the law of attraction: what you "reflect" as feelings, energy, and emotion can and will influence your physical reality—As Above, So Below.

For these reasons and more, people have worshiped the moon and likened it to divine power and magic for thousands of years.

Throughout this book, you'll work with the moon to find your own rhythm and reflection of light. So... *look up... Look at the moon!*

THE SECRETS OF

YOUR FEELINGS ARE THE SECRET SAUCE

To make real magic happen, combine actions (things that you do), intentions (also known as feelings or emotions), as well as powers outside of yourself, such as the moon and nature. This chart will give you some ideas on how to feel and set your intentions, while the next chart will cover actions. Both are essential ingredients to make your magic come alive.

An intention is when you strongly feel what you desire in your body, as if you already have it. And as the moon waxes and wanes, you'll "pull the thread" of magic forward by listening to your feelings and continually refocusing these intentions with actions to match.

Since the moon and emotions are both linked to the subconscious, *you'll use your body to feel these things and set intentions,* not your thoughts in your conscious mind.

First Quarter
Feel where you would like to change, grow, or expand. Allow yourself to dream and imagine what it might be like to make a change, even if it doesn't seem possible right now.

Waxing Crescent
Feel what excites you and sparks a sense of curiosity. Ask questions and look for answers, clues, patterns, and coincidences. Use the subtle feelings of what "lights you up" to set intentions and guide your actions.

New Moon
Allow yourself to feel where you are judging yourself. When you are ready, forgive yourself and let the energy shift until you find a place of neutrality and self-acceptance.

MOON MAGIC

Full Moon
Reaffirm your visions and intentions until the energy of what you desire begins to feel real.
If you feel clarity, make decisions to move forward quickly. If you feel confusion, illuminate your emotions through writing, ritual, divination, movement, etc.
Ask: What am I missing? What am I feeling?

Last Quarter
Allow yourself to feel what's working, and what isn't. Let your feelings flow to a place of ease and trust in yourself, so you can discern what you want and what you do not want.

Waning Crescent
Feel the relief as you realize that some thoughts and feelings are unnecessary. Intend to let those things go, and then see what you have left. Let your intentions flow to a place of release.

Dark Moon
Let the darkness filter out noise and distractions. Take a step back from actions and thoughts. Allow the dark moon to reset your mind, body, and spirit with the energy of rest.

Patchouli

Waxing Gibbous
This nearly-full moon is a powerful time to look closely at your plans for the moon phase and refine them. Cast spells for personal power, strength, and tenacity. Keep going. You've got this!

Nettle & Mint

First Quarter
A beautiful moon to take action, draw in lunar power, and cast spells to increase whatever you desire more of in your life.

Citrine

Waxing Crescent
Follow your curiosity to explore new things. Begin activities to transform yourself and grow.

Sage

New Moon
The time just before the first light of the moon is auspicious for new beginnings. Cast spells to start new things, refresh your altar or physical space, and dream, plan, or discover new desires and possibilities.

Thyme & Salt

START HERE
Rose Quartz - Self Love

MOON PHASES

MOON SPELLS

You can do powerful spells!

MOON WATER

Place water under the full or new moon. Add crystals, herbs, and oils if desired. Use this water to anoint yourself or your tools in ritual.

Fill a black or silver bowl with water

Or gaze at the surface of a lake, puddle, or calm sea

SCRYING & DIVINATION

Read tarot cards, gaze at the moon, or gaze at the reflection of the moon on water. Look for visual clues, patterns, or flashes of inspiration.

Start simply! *Use your talents!*

ALTAR & CORRESPONDENCE

An altar is a place to bring the spiritual into the material world—As Above, So Below. Symbolism amplifies your magic and speaks to your subconscious on a deeper level than words or thoughts. Discover symbolism that represents the full "you," dark and light—the true essence of yourself.

Incense & Oils

Use scents and the magical properties of herbs to help you visualize, clarify, release, and otherwise add power to your spells.

MOON BATHING

Bathe or shower (pour the ritual water over your head) to calm, cleanse, or energize your mind, body, and spirit.

AND RITUALS

Candle Spells

Simply gaze at a candle flame, or use candles to enhance and energize your magic. Customize your candles with oils, herbs, colors, and carvings.

Try moon magic tonight!

TEA & KITCHEN

Eat, drink, and be magical! Add magic to your daily life and use non-toxic herbs for teas, cooking rituals, and kitchen spells.

MANIFESTING & RELEASING

Use the new, waxing, and full moon phases to visualize and work towards what you wish to manifest or create in your life.

Use the full, waning, and dark moons to release, let go, connect to your intuition, and create space for change to manifest.

CLEARING & CHARGING

Use the moon's magic to calm or energize yourself, your ritual tools, your crystals, or your spells.

MEDITATION

Use the moon's phases to accept the ups and downs of life, and to connect to your intuition, deities, or inner wisdom.

Eat or burn basil leaves to gather courage.

Wear or carry a citrine crystal to amplify your manifestations.

Stir clockwise during the waxing or full moon to create forward momentum.

Moon Spells in Action
Manifesting With the Moon

Magic is often defined as the ability to influence your life through intention and will—but there is another essential part—action.

Keep in mind that action doesn't have to be...active. Rest and reflection are parts of the moon's cycle, so they're important steps for you, too.

You can use the moon's phases to create and manifest what you desire, gently "stirring the cauldron" in a continuous manner.

For a physical mechanism to help you along, focus on the intentions behind your spellwork as you stir your coffee or tea. Stir clockwise during the waxing and full moon, and counterclockwise during the waning and dark moon.

Watch how your stirring keeps spinning, even when you stop the action. This is just like periods of rest and reflection—the actions you've taken keep the spell moving—so there's no need to worry if you take a break or stop to reflect.

The spells in this book will go into more detail on how to use each moon phase, but here is a general recap to get you started:

DARK & NEW MOON: Get introspective. Choose what you desire and ask, "What's next?"

WAXING MOON: After the new moon, start putting new things in motion. Use what you learned during the last waning moon to guide you.

FULL MOON: When the full moon arrives, go over what you've accomplished and give yourself some credit. Celebrate your actions and magic.

WANING MOON: During the waning moon and into the dark moon, take time to rest, read, research, journal, and go inward. Learn & reflect on whatever you're working on with your spells.

REPEAT: Repeat this cycle continuously to keep motion going between learning, resting, and taking actions. You'll "stir the cauldron" and keep your magic flowing with the power of the moon.

YOUR MOON QUEST

Choose what you desire. This is your MOON QUEST. Use the following prompts to write down actions, feelings, things to do, and "ways of being" that align with the goal of your MOON QUEST. Use the seasonal correspondences for long-term projects.

NEW MOON ACTIVITIES AND GOALS
(ALSO CORRESPONDS TO JANUARY & FEBRUARY)

How can you follow your curiosities, know yourself better, and start in a new direction, physically and energetically?

WAXING MOON ACTIVITIES AND GOALS
(ALSO CORRESPONDS TO MARCH, APRIL, AND MAY)

How can you take action and feel empowered? What do you need to feel and do to make your dreams and spells come true?

FULL MOON ACTIVITIES AND GOALS
(ALSO CORRESPONDS TO JUNE AND JULY)

How can you experience the fullest version of who you are right now?

WANING MOON ACTIVITIES AND GOALS
(ALSO CORRESPONDS TO AUGUST, SEPTEMBER, OCTOBER)

What can you release? How can you allow ease and trust in yourself?

DARK MOON ACTIVITIES AND GOALS
(ALSO CORRESPONDS TO NOVEMBER & DECEMBER)

How can you rest and go within? What can you do to refresh?

the correspondence of THE MOON AND SEASONS

The moon completes a full cycle of its phases in just over 28 days, which is relatively quick. One moon cycle is perfect for shorter projects and immediate goals.

This book also relates the moon phases to a longer-term cycle, the seasons, also known as the Wheel of the Year, so you can use this longer cycle for longer-term goals and plans that'll take more than a month.

While the seasons and sun embody more of a conscious or outward energy, the moon is subconscious or internal. However, they both follow a similar cycle and progression of dark to light.

The handy chart on the following page demonstrates that the phases of the moon correspond to a similar energy point in the Wheel of the Year. This similar pattern of energy—the waxing and waning of light—is no coincidence. It's the pattern and flow of the creative force of the universe. This process and cycle is how magic "works" and what you'll cycle with in this book.

Here's an overview of the eight sabbats and a chart that connects them to the moon phases and seasons.

IMBOLC: February 1 or 2. Imbolc is the time to celebrate the first signs of spring, or the return of the sun's increasing light. This sabbat corresponds to the waxing crescent moon.

OSTARA: March 20. This sabbat is celebrated on the spring equinox. Witches often mark this day with a ritual planting of seeds. Ostara corresponds to the first quarter moon.

BELTANE: May 1. Beltane is a time for rituals of growth, creation, and taking action to make things happen. This sabbat corresponds to the waxing gibbous moon.

LITHA: June 20. This sabbat celebrates the summer solstice, when the sun is at its strongest. Litha is a time of great magical and personal power and corresponds to the full moon.

LUGHNASADH: August 1. This day is a celebration of the "first harvest" where we gather early grains, herbs, fruits, and vegetables from the earth. It corresponds to the waning gibbous moon, where light and power begin to descend from their fullest stage.

MABON: September 21. Celebrated on the autumnal equinox, this sabbat is about release, balance, and letting go. It is the second harvest and corresponds to the last quarter moon.

SAMHAIN: October 31. Samhain is a celebration of the dark half of the year. It is a time to cast spells of protection for the upcoming winter. It corresponds to the waning crescent moon.

YULE: December 21. Marked by the winter solstice and the shortest (darkest) day of the year, this sabbat corresponds to the dark and new moon.

A NOTE ABOUT THE CROSS QUARTER DATES AND SOUTHERN HEMISPHERE:

CROSS QUARTER DATES: The dates for the two solstices and two equinoxes each year—Ostara, Litha, Mabon, and Yule—are calculated astronomically, from the position of the earth to the sun. The "cross quarter" festivals, which are the points between—Imbolc, Beltane, Lughnasadh, and Samhain—are often celebrated on "fixed" dates instead of the actual midpoints. Choose either date or any time in between for your own ritual. 'Tis the season for magic.

SOUTHERN HEMISPHERE SEASONS: If you're on the "southern" half of the Earth, like in Australia, the seasonal shifts are opposite on the calendar year. So you'll feel the energy of the summer solstice (corresponding to the full moon) in December instead of June, and so on.

SOUTHERN HEMISPHERE MOONS: The moon phase is the same for the whole planet, however the moon "looks" opposite in the southern hemisphere—waxing moons face right and waning moons face left. The illustrations in this book depict the northern hemisphere moon.

MOON SIGNS
The Moon in the Zodiac

Alongside the moon's phases, our moon also travels through the twelve zodiac constellations approximately every 28 days.

The moon transits through each individual zodiac sign for about two or three days. You can use these short cycles to hyper-focus your magic and intentions, if you wish.

You'll often hear the moon sign called out (full moon in Scorpio!)

Use these pages as a handy reference sheet to see if you can feel the intricacies of the moon as it transits through the zodiac signs.

MOON IN ARIES

A fire sign, the moon in Aries evokes a desire to start fresh. You may find you've got extra energy to get things done and start new projects. However, this moon is a better time to start (and complete) short-term projects rather than long-term projects or planning. Channel energy or frustrations into movement and child-like activities—art, sports, or other playful activities that you enjoy.

MOON IN TAURUS

An earth sign and the zodiac sign symbolizing the home, comfort, decor, and finances. The moon in Taurus is an optimal moon sign for starting long-term projects. You may feel called to spend time at home, in your garden, or in nature. This moon sign is an excellent time to ground yourself by meditating or contemplating your desires outdoors.

MOON IN GEMINI

An air sign, the moon in Gemini is an excellent time for thinking, learning, reading, pursuing curiosities and interests, focusing on mental activities, traveling, and talking with fascinating people. You may find that journaling or discussing deep topics with others will lead to rewarding insights and new perspectives when the moon is in Gemini.

MOON IN CANCER

A water sign, the moon in Cancer is a time to be at home, reflect, and get in touch with your feelings. You may feel called to focus on bonding with family or loved ones in intimate ways. Cooking and cleaning may be more appealing when the moon is in Cancer. Activities in or near water, like swimming or walking along the shore, can help you get in tune with your watery emotions.

MOON IN LEO

A fire sign, the moon in Leo is a time to focus on yourself and your creativity. It's a magical time to get in touch with your own intuition and listen for what your heart truly desires. Do, say, and be who you are without fear. Let yourself shine and take time to live, laugh, and love as passionately as you can. This moon sign can be an excellent time for dating. However, you may also prefer to spend it all on yourself.

MOON IN VIRGO

Virgo is the earth sign associated with organization, efficient habits, and health. A moon in Virgo is undoubtedly the best time to start a new routine or positive habit, or to organize, get on a schedule, or tidy things up. You may find that your mind is sharp, sensitive, and quick while the moon is in Virgo, so take this opportunity to catch up on your studies, read, or learn new things.

MOON IN LIBRA

An air sign of diplomacy, balance, and visual appeal. The moon in Libra can be an auspicious time to work on relationships, find balance, and socialize. You may also be called to let some things go, to regain harmony or release the weight of what holds you down while the moon is in Libra. The Libra moon is also a time to speak up, share, or write about topics you believe in.

MOON IN SCORPIO

A dark water sign, use the moon in Scorpio to "find" motivation, harness your own power, take control, and rid yourself of things that no longer serve you. You may find you've got the drive and power to work on your finances or speak your mind on things you typically are afraid to bring up. Use this moon time to pursue any of your passions or go deep into topics of importance.

MOON IN SAGITTARIUS

The fire sign of truth and visions, the moon in Sagittarius is a time to make long-term plans that take you in new directions, to think big, to use your imagination, and visualize a positive future. You may also want to plan a trip, do something you've always wanted to do, or speak your truth where you've held back.

MOON IN CAPRICORN

An earth sign, the moon in Capricorn is a time to focus on career, business, structure, careful use of resources, and practical achievement. You may also feel inspired to declutter, get rid of energy and possessions you no longer need, or to otherwise cut the excess and reprioritize what is truly important in your life.

MOON IN AQUARIUS

An air sign that symbolizes esoterica, freethinking, and personal freedom, the moon in Aquarius is an excellent time to expand your mind to find new, unexpected ideas and solutions. Think about what you can do to help humanity or how you can contribute to society. If you typically follow the pack, this is an auspicious time to go your own way.

MOON IN PISCES

The water sign of dreaming, psychic awareness, and intuition, the moon in Pisces is auspicious time for divination, reflection, mystical pursuits, and retreats into nature or water. The two fish of this sign signify the pull of our earthy desires vs. our spiritual pursuits, so take time to balance this with meditation, daydreaming, and getting in touch with your soul's calling.

Spellcasting Basics

There are opening and closing steps that are basic accompaniments to spells in this book. These steps are optional but advisable: at least know "why" many witches perform these processes and try them out for yourself.

And keep in mind, this is a super basic "coloring book" guide to the spellcasting process. There are books and online sources that go much further in-depth.

THE SECRET OF SPELLS

The secret to powerful spells is in you. Your feeling and vibration in alignment with your true source of self—and/or a higher power—is what makes spells work.

The secret isn't in having the right ingredients and doing all the steps in a particular order. It's in your ability to focus your intent and use your feelings, mind, and soul to call in what you want—to harness the energy of yourself in harmony with the Earth, stars, moon, planets, or whatever other spiritual forces you call upon.

BREAK THE RULES

The first rule is to throw out any of the rules that don't work for you. Do things that feel right, significant, and meaningful. Adapt spells from different practices, books, and teachers. The only way to know what works is to follow your curiosity and try things out.

USING TOOLS

Your feelings and vibration are what unlocks the magic, not the tools, exact words, or sequences. You can cast amazing spells for free with no tools at all, and you can cast an elaborate spell that yields no results.

That said, tools like herbs, oils, crystals, and cauldrons can be powerful and fun to use in your spells. Just don't feel pressured or discouraged if you don't have much to start. Keep your magic straightforward and powerful. The right tools and ingredients will come.

"AS ABOVE, SO BELOW"

Tools, ingredients, and symbols are based on the magical theory of sympathetic magic and correspondence. You might hear the phrase, "As Above, So Below," which means the spiritual qualities of objects are passed down to earth. It's "sympathetic magic," or "this equals that," like how a figure of a lion represents that power but is not an actual lion.

Start by following lists, charts, and spells to get a feel for what others use and then begin to discover your own meaningful symbolism and correspondences.

PERMISSION

Spellbooks are like guidelines. They should be modified, simplified, or embellished to your liking. And don't degrade your magic by calling it "lazy." Keeping your witchcraft simple is okay. Go ahead, you have permission.

Also, it's not a competition to see who can use the most esoteric stuff in their spell. Hooray! It's about finding your personal power and style.

SPELLCASTING OUTLINE:
1. Plan and prepare.
2. Cast a circle.
3. Ground and center.
4. Invoke a deity or connection to self.
5. Raise energy.
6. Do your spellcraft (like the spells in this book).
7. Ground and center again.
8. Close your circle.
9. Clean up.
10. Act in accord (and be patient!).

1. PLAN AND PREPARE: If you're doing a written spell, read it several times to get familiar with it. Decide if there's anything you'll substitute or change. If you're writing your own spell, enjoy the process and mystery of seeing the messages and theme come together.

Gather all of the items you'll be using (if any) and plan out space and time where you'll do the spell. Spells can be impromptu, so preparations can be quick and casual if you like.

2. CAST A CIRCLE AND CALL THE QUARTERS: A magic circle is a container to collect the energy of your spell. Circles are also protective, as they form a ring or "barrier" around you. Circles can elevate your space to a higher vibration and clear out unwanted energy before you begin. Calling the Quarters is done to get the universal energy of the elements flowing. Incense is typically burned at the same time to purify the air and energy. If you can't burn things, that's ok. If you've never cast a circle, try it. It's a mystical experience like no other. Once you have a few candles lit and start to walk around it, magic does happen!

HOW TO CAST A CIRCLE: This is a basic, bare-bones way to cast a circle. It's often much more elaborate, and this explanation barely does it justice, so read up to find out more. And note that while some cast the circle first and then call the Quarters, some do it the other way around.

1. Hold out your hand, wand, or crystal, and imagine a white light and a sphere of pure energy surrounding your space, as you circle around clockwise three times. Your circle can be large or it can be tiny, just space for you and your materials.

2. Call the Four Quarters or Five Points of the Pentagram, depending on your preferences. The Quarters (also known as the Elements!) are Earth (North), Air (East), Fire (South), and Water (West). Many use the Pentagram and also call the 5th Element, Spirit or Self.

Face in each direction and say a few words to welcome the element. For example, "To the North, I call upon your power of grounding and strength. To the East, I call upon the source of knowledge. To the South, I call upon your passion and burning desire to take action. To the West, I call upon the intuition of emotion. To the Spirit and Source of Self, I call upon your guidance and light."

3. GROUND AND CENTER: Grounding and centering prepare you to use the energy from the Earth, elements, and universe. Most witches agree that if you skip these steps, you'll be drawing off of your own energy, which can be exhausting and ineffective. It's wise to ground and center both before and after a spell. It's like the difference between being "plugged into" the magical energy of the Earth and universe versus "draining your batteries."

HOW TO GROUND AND CENTER:
To ground, imagine the energy coming up from the core of the Earth and into your feet, as you breathe deeply. You can visualize deep roots from your feet all the way into the center of the Earth, with these roots drawing the Earth's energy in and out of you. The point is to allow these great channels of energy to flow through you and into your spell. You can also imagine any of your negative energy, thoughts, or stress leaving.

To center, once you've got a good flow of energy from the ground, imagine the energy shining through and out the top of your head as a pure form of your highest creative self and then back in as the light of guidance. Suspend yourself here between the Earth and the sky, supported with the energy flowing freely through you, upheld, balanced, cleansed, and "in flow" with the energy of the universe. This process takes just a couple of minutes.

4. INVOKE A DEITY OR CREATIVE SOURCE: If you'd like to invoke a deity or your highest self to help raise energy and your vibration, call upon them. Invoking deities is way deeper than this book, so research it more if it calls to you!

5. RAISE ENERGY: The point of raising energy is to channel the universal (magical!) forces you tapped into through the previous steps to use in your spell. And raising energy is fun. You can sing, dance, chant, meditate, or do breath work. You want to do something that feels natural, so you can really get into it, lose yourself, and raise your state of consciousness.

A good way to start is to chant "Ong," allowing the roof of your mouth to vibrate ever so slightly. This vibration changes up the energy in your mind, body, and breath and is a simple yet powerful technique.

Another tip is to raise energy to the point of the "peak" where you feel it at its highest. Don't go too far where you start to tucker out or lose enthusiasm!

6. DO YOUR SPELL: Your spell can be as simple as saying an intention and focusing on achieving the outcome of what you want, or it can be more elaborate. Whichever way you prefer, do what feels right to you.

TIPS ON VISUALIZATION AND INTENTION:
Most spellwork involves a bit of imagination and intention, and here are some subtleties you can explore.

The Power of You The most important tool in magic is you. You've got it—both power right now and vast untapped power that you can explore. To cast a successful spell, you've got to focus your mind and genuinely feel the emotions and feelings of the things you want to manifest.

If you haven't started meditating in some form yet, start now! It's not too late, and it's easier than you think.

Visualize the Outcome
Visualization doesn't have to be visual. In fact, *feeling* the outcome of what you want may be more effective than seeing it (try both). And try to feel or see the *completion* of your desire without worrying about the process or *how* you'll get there.

If you don't know how you're going to achieve your goal (yet!) it can feel overwhelming when you try to visualize how you're going to pull it off. Instead, feel the sense of calm, completion, and control that you'll feel *after* you achieve it.

Phrase it Positively
Another tip is to phrase your intentions and desires positively. You're putting energy into this, so make sure the intention is going to be good for you. Instead of saying what you don't want, "to get out of my bad job that I hate," phrase it positively, "I want to do something that's fulfilling with my career."

Then you'll be able to feel good about it as you visualize and cast your spell.

7. GROUND AND CENTER AGAIN

After your spell, it's important to ground out any excess energy. Do this again by visualizing energy flowing through you and out. You can also imagine any "extra" energy you have petering out as you release it back into the Earth.

8. CLOSE YOUR CIRCLE

If you called the Quarters or a deity, let them know the spell has ended by calling them out again, with thanks if desired.

Close your circle the opposite of how you opened it, circling around three times or more counterclockwise. Then say, "This circle is closed," or do a closing chant or song to finish your spell.

9. CLEAN UP

Don't be messy with your magic! Put away all of your spell items.

10. ACT IN ACCORD: Once you have cast your spell, you've got to take action. You can cast a spell to become a marine biologist, but if you don't study for it, it's never going to happen. So take action towards what you want to open the possibility for it to come.

Look for signs, intuition, and coincidences that point you in the direction of your desires. If you get inspired after a spell, take action! Don't be surprised if you ask for money and then come up with a new idea to make money. Follow those clues, especially if they feel exciting and good.

If your spell comes true, discard and "release" any charm bag, poppet, or item you used to hold and amplify energy. Also, give thanks (if that's in your practice) or repay the universe in some way, doing something kind or of service that you feel is a solid trade for what you received from your spell.

WHAT IF YOUR SPELL DOESN'T WORK?

It's true that not all spells will work! But sometimes the results just take longer than you'd like, so be patient.

If your spell doesn't work, you can use divination or meditation to do some digging into reasons why.

The good news is your own magic, power, frequency, and intention is still on your side. You can try again and add more energy in the direction of your desired outcome by casting another spell.

Give it some deep thought. What else is at play? Did you really take inspired action? Are you totally honest with yourself about what you want? Are there any thoughts or feelings about your spell that feel "off"? Are you grateful for what you already have? Can you "give back" or reciprocate with service or energy?

FOR MORE TIPS AND INSPIRATION:

Seek out websites, books, podcasts, and videos on spirituality. Follow your intuition and curiosity to deepen your practice and find your own style. And check out other books in the *Coloring Book of Shadows* series, like the *Book of Spells* and *Witch Life*.

SOUTHERN HEMISPHERE MAGIC

If you're in the Southern Hemisphere in a place like Australia, there are a couple of differences that you'll need to note.

The biggest difference is that since seasonal shifts are opposite on the calendar year, you'll feel the energy of Samhain around May 1 instead of October 31.

Southern Hemisphere "spinning and circle casting" will go "sun wise" according to the south—counterclockwise for invoking (drawing in), clockwise for banishing (letting go).

North and South Elements are also typically swapped in Southern Hemisphere magic— North = Fire, South = Earth.

So Mote it Be.

"HIS MOTHER WAS A WITCH, AND ONE SO STRONG THAT COULD CONTROL THE MOON."

William Shakespeare
The Tempest, Act V

# What is your New Moon intention?

The 9 "moon scenes" (facing page) are a riff on the 15th century Book of Hours, Très Riches Heures du Duc de Berry

What symbolizes the New Moon to you?

Burn juniper, cedar, and lemon balm to call on the energy of Artemis.

What Spells & Actions Feel Right to You During This Moon Phase?

Triple Goddess
MAIDEN-MOTHER-CRONE

The phases of life and of the moon

What do you experience while performing this spell?

Celestite - Inner peace & the guidance within

New Moon Magic
A Ritual to Start Fresh

Perform this ritual on any new moon of the year or on the full moon in January.

The new moon is a time to start fresh and allow yourself to begin again.

This moon phase corresponds to the month of January or deep winter. The energy of this season and moon suggests a desire for change, which becomes possible from a place of self-acceptance.

And that's the paradox of new beginnings: you're wishing for newness, but you won't find the power to change in something new. Your power is in the feeling of belonging just as you are, without changing a thing about yourself.

THINGS YOU'LL NEED: A dark space to sit in silence, outdoors if possible. Optional: Thirteen candles set in a circle to represent each of the moons for the year, or five candles for the elements air, earth, fire, water, and spirit. Earthy incense such as patchouli, cypress, or verbena.

CAST THE SPELL: Light your incense if desired. Allow yourself a moment in the pitch darkness. This darkness is a space where there is nothing to do, nothing to change, and nothing to fix. Imagine yourself floating in the darkness, slowing moving towards the feeling of self-acceptance. There is a part of the universe that wholly supports, loves, and cares for you, just as you are. Be patient—you will find it.

If you're using candles, light them one at a time in a clockwise manner, with the light of each candle amplifying the acceptance of yourself.

When you feel a shift to a sense of peace within yourself, you are ready for whatever you desire to do or be next.

What is your Waxing Crescent intention?

What symbolizes the Waxing Crescent to you?

WAXING CRESCENT SYMBOLS
Increasing Energy · Growth · Taking Action

WHAT SPELLS & ACTIONS FEEL RIGHT TO YOU DURING THIS MOON PHASE?

What do you experience while performing this spell?

- Pentacle -
The power of the Elements

- Keys -
A symbol of possibility

FIRE: What new actions do you want to take?

WATER: What new feelings do you want to feel?

AIR: What new thoughts do you want to think?

EARTH: What new habits do you want to create?

SPIRIT: What is your soul calling you to do?

Waxing Crescent Moon
A Sliver of Light

Do this work on any waxing crescent moon or on the full moon in February (mid-winter).

The waxing crescent, when the moon's first sliver of light emerges, symbolizes the power of possibility and the magic of starting new things. This moon reminds us that nothing is permanent. You've always got the power to change.

The keys to unlocking "what's next" are often hidden "in the shadows." Perhaps you were called to art, spirituality, or botany, but you've buried those interests out of fear or to protect yourself.

Or maybe you're aware of these keys, but they seem like a random pile of shiny objects. Trust that they're not random. These pieces, parts, and shiny things all have a place in your life.

In this spell, you'll make an elemental key to guide you towards the new things you desire.

PREPARE: First, answer the "pentagonal key" questions on the facing page. Don't overthink it. Trust your first inclinations without letting judgment or "the shadows" block the light.

Procure an actual key, or just write your answers on paper and use the paper as your key.

CAST THE SPELL: Hold your key under the moonlight until you feel the moonbeams shine within you. Then speak the answers to your key to set your intention. Anoint your key (optional) with a drop of basil oil or a sprig of basil.

Place the key under your pillow and sleep on it each night until the next full moon. Then keep your key in a special place—on your altar, in a charm bag, hung on the wall, around your neck, or blowing in the wind outdoors. This key will serve as an amulet of focus and power.

What is your First Quarter intention?

What symbolizes the First Quarter to you?

What spells & actions feel right to you during this moon phase?

Sip ginger and citrus tea to ignite your spirit, enliven your senses, and stoke the fire of action.

What do you experience while performing this spell?

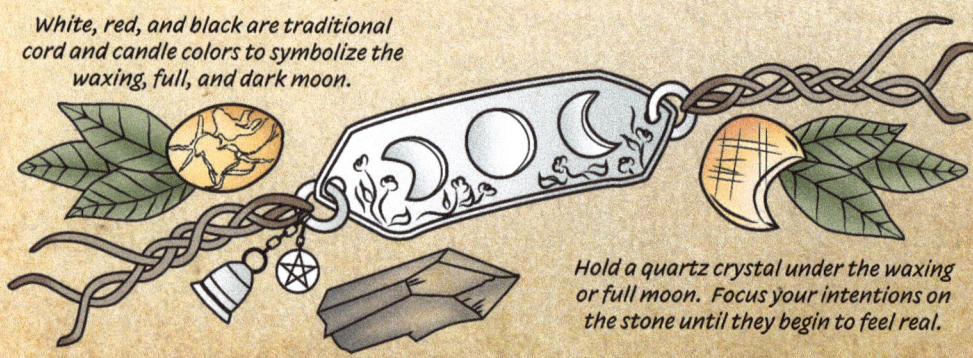

White, red, and black are traditional cord and candle colors to symbolize the waxing, full, and dark moon.

Hold a quartz crystal under the waxing or full moon. Focus your intentions on the stone until they begin to feel real.

First Quarter Moon
A Knot Spell to Harness the Moon's Power

Perform this spell on a waxing moon, or on the full moon in March (early spring).

The waxing first-quarter moon embodies the energy of increasing power. This moon marks an auspicious time to focus your actions, nurture relationships, or "grow" whatever you wish.

Witches have used knot spells for hundreds (possibly thousands) of years. In Celtic lore, knots represent tying and untying of elemental powers, binding intention to the knot's creator.

THINGS YOU'LL NEED: A three-foot cord, one strand or three strands braided. Saltwater and an oil such as myrrh, olive, or eucalyptus.

CAST THE SPELL: Under the light of the moon, purify the cord with a sprinkle of saltwater, then anoint it with a drop of oil. Hold your cord up to the moon. Feel the lunar energy and light shining onto it and through your hands.

You'll tie either nine or thirteen knots into the cord, representing the nine phases of the moon or the thirteen moons of the year (your choice!).

Start with the first knot, and as you tie it, hold it up so you can see the moon through the loop that the knot creates. As you pull it closed, envision the moon power tying into the cord. Repeat for all but one knot, tying as evenly spaced as you can. For the 9th or 13th knot, tie the two ends together, or leave it as one strand.

To use your moon cord, drape it around yourself or place it on your altar. Its presence will remind you of the power you have to change or create whatever you desire. You can also untie the knots when you need extra moon power. Repeat the spell and re-tie it to charge it again.

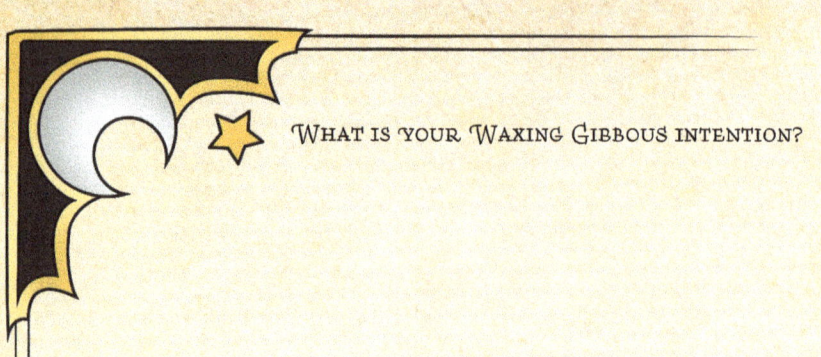

What is your Waxing Gibbous intention?

- Sprouts -
Energy manifesting in the physical realm

- Beryl -
Confidence in beginning new things

What symbolizes the Waxing Gibbous Moon to you?

WHAT SPELLS & ACTIONS FEEL RIGHT TO YOU DURING THIS MOON PHASE?

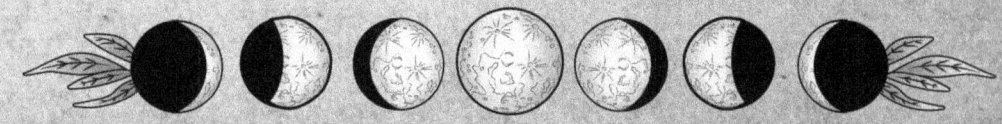

WHAT DO YOU EXPERIENCE WHILE PERFORMING THIS SPELL?

Cast a circle with rose petals, elder flowers, or hawthorn blossoms for protection and spiritual energy.

- Patchouli -
Witch Power

Waxing Gibbous Moon
A Moon Mirror for Personal Power

Perform this spell during the waxing gibbous moon phase or on any full moon.

The waxing and full moons hold powerful energy. You can harness this moon magic by charging a "moon mirror." Moons and mirrors (or reflective surfaces like water or polished stone) have been used in magic for millennia. The moon's light is a reflection of the sun, as the moon produces no light of its own. And so, reflections are a potent form of moon magic.

THINGS YOU'LL NEED: A small round mirror. You can also use a polished stone or piece of metal. A container for the mirror that will obscure it from light, such as a dark cloth, bag, or box. If desired, embellish the container with embroidery, paint, or beads in lunar designs. A dark place and time where you can directly view the moon. An optional anointing oil or herb for power such as patchouli, cinquefoil, or mugwort.

PERFORM THE SPELL: With your mirror at the ready, cast a circle under the waxing or full moon's light. Hold the mirror up so you can see the moon reflected within. Rotate the mirror clockwise, either 3, 5, 9, or 13 times.

Use a drop of oil or sprig of herb and rub all the way around the edge of the mirror, clockwise, to consecrate and seal the spell. The mirror will be charged with the moon's power.

Place the mirror in the container, and do not let it see the light of day until you are ready to use it. When you're in need of personal power, intuitive guidance or resilience, gaze at your reflection in the mirror. Once you've used the mirror's magic, recharge it at the next waxing or full moon.

WHAT IS YOUR FULL MOON INTENTION?

- Cinquefoil & St. John's Wort -
Elemental Power

WHAT SYMBOLIZES THE FULL MOON TO YOU?

What spells & actions feel right to you during this moon phase?

WHAT SPELLS & ACTIONS FEEL RIGHT TO YOU DURING THIS MOON PHASE?

What do you experience while performing this spell?

Write your favorite moon chant in the space on the left.

The Full Moon
Ritual of Drawing Down the Moon

One of the most iconic full moon rituals is "Drawing Down the Moon." In theory, this simplified version of the ritual takes you to a trance state where you'll allow the moon goddess, god, or energy of the moon to be present within you.

If your practice is more secular or you aren't comfortable channeling a deity, you can call on the moon's energy as intuition, universal wisdom, or the power of your own divinity.

THINGS YOU'LL NEED: Plan to do this ritual under the light of the full moon. Going outdoors where you can see the moon is best, but you can perform it indoors at a window if necessary.

The only tool you need is your own body and spirit. However, many witches like to do this ritual with a tool—charging the tool with more moon power each time they perform it. This tool could be a crystal, a bowl or chalice of water, something made of silver, or whatever item represents the moon to you.

PERFORM THE RITUAL: Stand under the moon's light, holding your tool (if applicable). Feel the earth's energy grounding you down, coming up through your body, and steadying your presence. Then, gaze at the moon (if you can't see it, imagine it) until you feel its energy flow through you, bringing you to a peaceful, trance-like state. It may help to chant. Pick a favorite chant or use the example a few pages back in this book.

Once you feel the fullness of the moon's power flowing through you, it's essential to let it shine back out. Visualize a bright orb coming out from the center of yourself and into a sphere around you, as if you have become the moon itself.

What do you experience while performing this spell?

Invigorate your moon bath or shower with bergamot, vetivert, and Epsom salt.

Harnessing the Full Moon
Working With Unwieldy Moon Energies

Have you ever felt sleepless, frustrated, or emotional at the full moon? Conversely, have you felt thrilled and bounding with energy?

The full moon typically amplifies what you've been feeling in the weeks prior, creating a surge of energy. While you can't control it, you can work with it. Here are a few ideas to try.

FOLLOW THE PHASES: No need to be perfect. A few actions each month make a big difference.

If you've rested as the moon waned and expressed yourself as it waxed, you may find that you are flowing with the full moon.

If you've pushed through the waning phase and stifled the waxing phase, you may feel frustrated.

MOVE SOME ENERGY: Go for a drive with the windows down, dance, breathe deeply, or sing.

FINISH UP: Clean your space and check things off your to-do list—especially things you've been putting off. This can help move stagnant energy.

EMOTE AND EXPRESS: Give a voice to your emotions—journal, paint, draw, talk, cry, yell—allow your emotional body to surface.

DIVINE AND REVEAL: Your intuition may be clearest at the full moon. Decision-making and divination can be highly effective at this time. Some believe the full moon is not a good time for decisions, but try it and see what you think.

BATHE: Epsom salt baths or swimming are fabulous ways to neutralize the moon's energy.

LET YOURSELF BE A LUNATIC: Literally. Go outside and scream, "I AM A LUNATIC!" Then cackle wildly (Trust! It's okay! Give it a try).

You may prefer to howl at the moon. This is also acceptable and highly encouraged.

If clouds obscure the full moon, think of an obstacle that you face. Gaze towards the moon until the clouds part, and you'll receive a moonbeam of inspiration.

What is your Waning Gibbous intention?

- Clary Sage & Rowanberry -
Enhancing psychic & intuitive powers.

What symbolizes the Waning Gibbous Moon to you?

What spells & actions feel right to you during this moon phase?

What do you experience while performing this spell?

Waning Gibbous Moon
Creating Magic with Moon Arts and Crafts

The moon has inspired the arts and human expression for thousands of years.

Any moon phase is a good time to make moon-art! But the waning gibbous moon can be extra special for crafting, as this moon is auspicious for studying, finding inspiration in nature, and discovering your sense of purpose—just like crafts.

CRAFT RITUALS: Set the intention of what you desire as you plan your moon-craft project. Find materials that symbolize your spellwork and manifestations for this next moon cycle.

As you craft, ask to channel the power and wisdom of the moon. Create in silence, or repeat a moon mantra, for example: *Dark to light, the power of the night. Wax and wane, release and gain.*

When finished, place your moon craft in a location of reverence, such as on your altar.

Stitch Witchery: Whether you sew, embroider, or do quilting, you can work moon-themed motifs, spirals, and lunar magic into anything you make. Experiment with "moon colors" and symbolism in silver, gold, and blue.

Jewelry and Adornments: Try your hand at beading with shiny moon crystals and lunar accouterments. Pearls, onyx, silver, quartz, and moonstone all symbolize the magic of the moon.

Stamps: Carve a potato with the triple moon, a spiral, or moon-phase motif. Then use fabric paint to stamp bands of lunar spellwork at the hems of dish towels, aprons, an altar cloth, special paper, clothing, or ritual tools.

Wreaths and Altar Decorations: Create lunar deity statues or other special symbolisms for your altar or to adorn a moon-shaped wreath.

WHAT IS YOUR LAST QUARTER INTENTION?

- Round fruits, gourds, & squash -
The abundance of the earth and the power of the moon.

What symbolizes the Last Quarter Moon to you?

Protect yourself from werewolves with aconite (wolfsbane).

WHAT SPELLS & ACTIONS FEEL RIGHT TO YOU DURING THIS MOON PHASE?

Chang'e
Chinese Goddess of the Moon

Honor Chang'e with round autumn nuts and fruits like hazelnuts, chestnuts, and persimmons.

What do you experience while performing this spell?

Tourmaline can help you accept where you might benefit from change.

Last Quarter Moon
Releasing with Moon Water

Do this work during any waning moon or on the full moon in September.

The last quarter moon holds a diminishing power. Change is hard, and the power of the waning moon's decaying energy can help make changes and releases a little easier. It's often the emotions of change that hurt. And since the moon corresponds to both water and emotions, these things together make for potent magic.

Write a list of the things you want to release—physically as well as emotionally—like thoughts, habits, resentments, mistakes, or patterns.

WITH TEARS: When performing these spells, allow yourself to deeply feel the emotions of letting go. Cry if possible—a release of water.

IN THE BATH: Soak while feeling or speaking what you wish to release. Feel the energy leave your body and absorb into the water. As the bath drains, let the emotions release along with it.

IN THE RAIN: Use white chalk to write what you wish to release on stones (or directly on the ground). Place the stones in the rain, then watch as the writing dissipates. Alternately, stand in the rain and allow the energy to wash away.

AT THE WATER'S EDGE: Gaze at the reflection of the waning moon on the water. Speak what you wish to release. Place your feet in the water and allow the energy to move through you, into the water, and to the reflection of the moon.

WITH A CHALICE: Fill a silver chalice with water. Light a candle. Speak the energies that you wish to release. Extinguish the flame in the chalice's water. Pour the water out at a crossroads or onto the bare earth.

What is your Waning Crescent intention?

- Owl -
Wisdom & Intuition

- Amber -
Forgiveness and trust in yourself

What symbolizes the Waning Crescent Moon to you?

WHAT SPELLS & ACTIONS FEEL RIGHT TO YOU DURING THIS MOON PHASE?

What do you experience while performing this spell?

FIRE: What actions make you feel heavy?

WATER: What emotions feel stuck and in need of release?

AIR: What unhelpful thoughts or beliefs are lurking in the shadow?

EARTH: What items or habits are holding you back?

SPIRIT: What have you been denying?

- Heather & Labradorite -
Spiritual protection and enlightenment

Waning Crescent Moon
Divination with the Crone

Do this "shadow work" on any waning crescent moon or on the full moon in October.

The waning crescent, the last sliver of light before the moon falls to darkness, is an auspicious time for delving into the shadow self, the subconscious, and all that is hidden beneath the surface. This moon represents the Crone goddess, the wisdom of the elder witch, or the wisdom of your own "elder" within.

While the previous spell dealt with emotions on the surface, we also hold emotions in the shadow. These are the things we have not yet felt or allowed ourselves to accept. Performing "shadow-work" can uncover what may lurk in the darkness of your own power.

THINGS YOU'LL NEED: Tarot cards or another form of divination (oracle cards, rune stones, a pendulum, the moon's reflection on water for scrying, or a notebook and pen to free-write).

Optional: Black candles. A dark incense such as frankincense, sloe berries, or cedar.

PERFORM THE SPELL: Walk, dance, or spiral counterclockwise (widdershins) and backwards. Or circle your hands widdershins until you feel your energy shift. You can greatly heighten the power of the ritual if you walk backwards on a wooded path, especially to a crossroads, but go slowly and use extreme caution if you do so.

As you circle or walk, chant:

Into the shadows to see the Crone.
While the night is dark, I am not alone.

Light your candle(s) and incense if desired. Then use your divination tool to ask the Crone the questions on the facing page.

DARK MOON

Rest and Renew

What is your Dark Moon intention?

WHAT SYMBOLIZES THE DARK MOON TO YOU?

DARK MOON SYMBOLS
REST · REGENERATE · RETREAT

Bat — Transformation through Darkness

Cypress — Immortality & the Cycle of Life and Death.

Jet

Acorns — A promise of renewal.

Blackthorn — Protection & Magic

Belladonna

Thorns & Brambles

— Skulls — Our Earthly Bodies

Hellebore — Banishing & Protection

Hecate — Greek Goddess of magic, the moon, and the darkness.

WHAT SPELLS & ACTIONS FEEL RIGHT TO YOU DURING THIS MOON PHASE?

What do you experience while performing this spell?

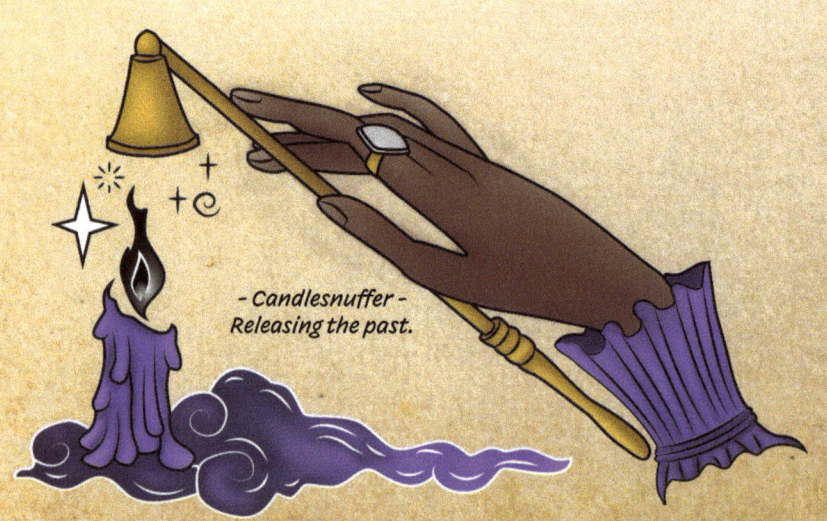

- Candlesnuffer -
Releasing the past.

The Dark Moon
A Classic "Cord Cutting" Ritual

Perform this spell during a dark moon, before any hint of the returning light of the new moon.

Cord cutting is a classic witch's rite, often performed to cut the ties between yourself and another person, most notably, a lover. However, you can use this ritual to "cut the cord" between yourself and whatever you wish to release.

The past two spells have dealt with letting go. While you may feel some relief and release—you might also still feel stuck on a thing or two, and that's okay. Some energies are hard to let go of, even when we desperately wish to let go. And the dark moon is the perfect void to release into.

THINGS YOU'LL NEED: Two small spell candles, colors of your choice. One to represent you, and one to represent the energy you wish to detach from. A length of natural twine (hemp, jute, cotton, or even a long length of dried grass). A fire-safe cauldron or location to burn things.

Perform this spell outside under the dark moon or indoors with the windows open.

CAST THE SPELL: Set up the two spell candles securely, a few inches from each other. Tie the twine around both of the candles several times, in a counterclockwise direction.

Then, light the candles. Allow them to burn down, burning the twine (the bond) along with them. Watch the candles and threads as they burn. Chant if you like, "The ties that bind, no longer mine. I release this bond, here and beyond."

Allow any memories or emotions to surface, then breathe them out towards the flame. Let the candles burn out. Bury any remnants of the spell in the ground or in a pot of earth.

What do you experience while performing this spell?

Burn sandalwood and lavender to enhance your spirit work.

Drink black tea with mugwort, thyme, and wormwood to heighten your psychic awareness.

The End is the Beginning
Finding the Wisdom in the Dark

The dark moon is a time to surrender to what is. This doesn't mean giving up, but letting go, and preparing for new possibilities when the light of the moon returns and the cycle begins again.

The energy of the dark moon suggests that there is wisdom in the space between the moons. There's a reason why the moon doesn't shine every night—the darkness is essential in magic.

THINGS YOU'LL NEED: A dark space to sit in silence. Thirteen candles set in a circle to represent each of the moons of the past year.

CAST THE SPELL: Light all thirteen candles, then cast your circle around them. Go within the circle, and allow yourself several moments of silence and meditation. Think about the year and the thirteen moons that have passed. The memories may still be strong in your mind, but in actuality, the past—even the recent past—no longer exists. It is done.

One by one, blow out each candle while you say or think a memory from your year. It's up to you whether they are your favorite memories, your least favorite, or a mix. Let them all neutralize.

Once all of the candles have been extinguished, allow yourself a moment in the pitch darkness. Then, just see what comes to you.

What are you feeling in the dark? What does it represent to you, both seasonally and personally? What is your relationship to the darkness? How would you like that to grow or change as the moon's light slowly returns?

After you've said your piece, listen deeply. What do you hear? What is the wisdom of the dark saying back to you?

Burn agrimony, hyssop, and vetivert to banish unwanted cycles and patterns.

Très Riches Heures du Duc de Berry

-

The Limbourg Brothers & their associates

-

15th Century

About the Artist

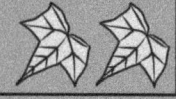

Amy Cesari

*and her familiars
Mr. Toad & Merlin*

Amy is an author and illustrator who loves animated musicals. She also likes watercolor painting, witchcraft, and walking on the beach in a really big sun hat.

Not only does she own every Nintendo game console ever made, she's earned several fancy diplomas and enjoys continued studies in various magical practices.

CONTACT AMY AND SEE MORE BOOKS, PRINTABLE PAGES, AND ART:
Amy@ColoringBookofShadows.com
ColoringBookofShadows.com

©2024 Amy Cesari, Book of Shadows LLC

www.ingramcontent.com/pod-product-compliance
Lightning Source LLC
Chambersburg PA
CBHW050729010526
44107CB00009B/790